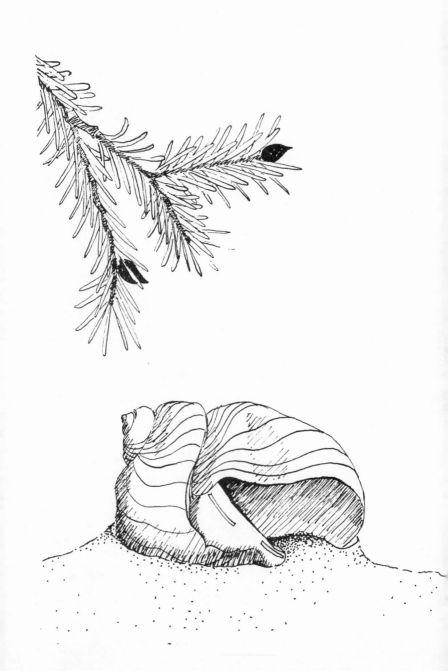

Parables for Little People

By Fr. Lawrence Castagnola, S.J.

 Resource Publications, Inc.
San Jose, California

"In memory of those children who are victims of war."

Book Design and Illustrations: Nancy LaBerge Muren
Typography: Virginia Sorich
Mechanical Layout: Stephen Weikart

Library of Congress Catalog Card Number 82-60029
ISBN: 0-89390-034-6

Contents

6

Foreword

THE TASK OF communicating the good news of Jesus to young children is a challenging undertaking. It requires not only a profound understanding of the words of Jesus and the teachings of the Church, but also an understanding of young children and the creative ability to communicate effectively with them.

Father Lawrence Castagnola, S. J., in "Parables for Little People," attempts to convey to young children basic truths of Christian behavior through the medium of the story. Creatively using his exceptional skills as a storyteller, Father Castagnola has for many years successfully helped young children to hear the good news in an ordinary and approachable way. It is my hope that you will find these stories helpful to the children in your life.

The story is a medium which can take certain liberty in its expression for the sake of effectively and powerfully communicating the Truth around which it is built. To make a search for the Truth is what Jesus came to inspire us to do. As the Scriptures tell us, Jesus is the Truth, and He is the Way to the Truth, and He is the Life which is experienced as a result of seeking the Truth. Father Castagnola's parables are intended to bring young children to a way of life which truthfully reflects the way of Jesus.

I gladly recommend these fresh and exciting stories to you and to your Little People.

Francis A. Quinn
Bishop of Sacramento

7

LaBerge Muren

Arnold
the
Elephant

ARNOLD THE ELEPHANT was born into a family of circus performers. His mother, dad and two brothers were the main event of the Peppermint Circus which traveled all over the world.

The Peppermint Elephants, as Arnold's family was called, did what was expected of circus elephants. When commanded by trainers they stood on their front legs or stood on their hind legs or held each others' tails with their trunks. But what made them special and world-famous was the fact that they could dance.

Arnold was clumsy. When he tried to stand on his front legs he fell on his face. When he tried to stand on his hind legs, he fell over on his back. He could never reach the tail of the elephant in front of him. And he dropped every rider he tried to lift on his back. Needless to say, he couldn't begin to dance. He was a Peppermint Elephant totally out of step.

The circus owner considered Arnold to be useless, and decided to sell him to the zoo. When Zero the clown heard of this plan, he went to the owner and begged him to let Arnold stay.

"Sir," said the clown, "Arnold is a klutz. We all know that. But you have to remember he is part of a family. And elephants are loyal. If you send him away, his brothers will rebel. Once they stampede, not all the tranquilizers in the veternarian's office will stop them."

The owner thought for a minute and then asked the clown, "But what am I to do with Arnold? All he does is eat and sleep. He is useless for our act. And with the rising cost of hay, I can't afford to feed him."

"I have an idea," said the clown. "I'll train Arnold to give the children rides during the intermission. All he has to do is walk back and forth. We'll put a large seat on him to hold six children. It will have a safety rail so no one will get hurt. At a dollar a ride, you will make a lot of money."

The owner liked the clown's idea. He liked the idea of making extra money. Arnold became an instant taxi for children.

On his first night of work Arnold gave rides for two hundred children. The owner was happy, the clown was happy, the children were happy and even the Peppermint Elephants were happy — except for Arnold. He was most unhappy.

He felt dumb being just a "ride" elephant. People cheered while his family danced. All he did was walk up and down a lane.

"Any elephant can give rides to children. I'll always be a no-good klutz." With these gloomy thoughts Arnold considered running away. But he didn't, realizing a creature his size couldn't very well hide in a neighborhood shopping center.

Seeing Arnold's unhappiness, Zero the clown took a personal interest in him. After each ride Arnold gave the children, he received a cube of sugar and a hug from Zero. Though Arnold couldn't speak with human words, he knew the sugar and hug meant he was loved and important.

Because of the clown's friendship, Arnold began to enjoy giving rides to the children. He no longer felt like a mechanical elephant. It was just when he was feeling good about himself that Zero the clown was laid off his job.

"With the price of food for my animals these days, I just can't keep all my clowns on the payroll," said the owner sadly.

In the days that followed Zero's departure, Arnold went back to his old ways of feeling sorry for himself. He ate less and lost his strength. During one of his rides he sat down and refused to move.

The circus owner realized Arnold was having problems because he had laid off Zero the clown. So he called Zero on the telephone.

"Zero, come quickly. Arnold needs you. You're re-hired."

Arnold was so happy to see Zero he almost did a dance. The clown gave Arnold a bag full of sugar cubes and a hug. Arnold got up and began giving rides again.

A few weeks after Zero's return, a great crash occurred at

the south end of the tent. A section of the stands had collapsed. People were screaming, and there was confusion everywhere. Zero kept his cool and took Arnold to where the stands had collapsed. A small boy named Patrick was pinned under a mass of splintered wood and twisted steel. The boy's parents were in a state of shock as they tried to help the circus hands lift the wreckage from their boy. But no human strength was able to budge the weight. After a hug from Zero, Arnold pushed his way to the boy. With an accurate swing of his trunk, he lifted the wreckage from the boy. Little Patrick smiled when he saw the elephant. He was all right, just frightened at being trapped.

Everyone stood in silent wonder at what Arnold had done. Zero took the microphone and said to the crowd, "This is the elephant who couldn't grab his brother's tail. This is the elephant who can't keep in step with his family. This is my friend, Arnold."

For most of the spectators it was the first time they had heard the ride-elephant's name. Most had been too busy during intermission buying cokes and cotton candy to even remember seeing Arnold. But with the clown's announcement they all began to chant, "Arnold, Arnold, three cheers for Arnold." If an elephant could turn pink from embarrassment, Arnold would have. He was not comfortable with people cheering for him. Shouts of approval were natural for the rest of his family, but not for the clumsy one, the klutz.

Thanks to Arnold, little Patrick was not hurt. The child begged his mom and dad to ride Arnold, and he rode his hero to the center of the ring with Zero leading the way.

In the days that followed his rescue performance, Arnold still could not learn his family act. Yet, he was happy with himself, and never for a moment thought it was a handicap to not be able to dance.

LaBerge Muren

14

The Rainbow People

I N A BEAUTIFUL meadow at the bottom of a great mountain lived a people called the "Greens." They wore green clothes, lived in green homes, drove green cars and believed that God was green.

At the top of the great mountain were another people, the "Blues." They wore blue clothes, lived in blue homes, drove blue cars and believed that God was blue.

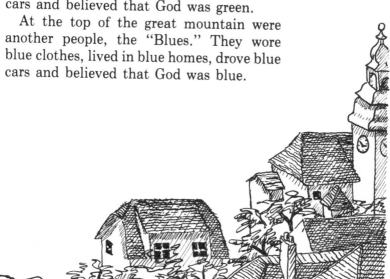

Greens and Blues didn't speak to each other. In fact they hated each other. Green parents would teach their children to say:

"Green is happy;
Blue is sad.
Greens are good;
Blues are bad."

Blue parents would teach their children to say, "Blue is happy; Green is sad. Blues are good, Greens are bad."

Blues and Greens grew up seeing each other as "sad" and "bad." But they didn't really know each other. Some Blues went a whole lifetime without even talking to a Green. They didn't know each other because they stayed in their own territories. They didn't go to the same churches or schools.

It happened one day that a Green boy was walking with his father when he saw a Blue boy flying his kite in their meadow. When the Blue boy saw them he became frightened. He ran back towards his mountain. But in doing so he sprained his ankle and couldn't walk very well. The Green boy wanted to help him, but his father said, "No."

"Don't you remember what your mother and I taught you? Green is happy; Blue is sad. Greens are good; Blues are bad."

The Green boy still asked his dad if he could help the Blue. "Dad, how do we know this Blue is bad? All I know is that he has a sprained ankle and he needs someone to help him walk home."

When the Green boy said this, his father turned to him saying: "Blue is the color of the devil. God only loves Green. Our religion teaches us to help our own kind. I want you to do as you are told."

A few weeks later the Green boy was out playing with his pet rabbit. He chased it through the tall grass and into the open fields. He played for so long that without realizing it, he had crossed into Blue Land. He was about to catch the rabbit when the rascal jumped down a small cliff. Green went after him and in so doing caught his right leg between two big rocks. He pushed and pulled, but could not move. He called for help hoping a Green would hear him. He worried that sooner or later a Blue would come by. This thought frightened him because he had never met a Blue.

As the sunlight faded, someone approached the trapped Green boy. It was a Blue. It was the same boy who had sprained his ankle, the boy who had been flying his kite in Green Land. The Green boy closed his eyes waiting to be hurt by his enemy.

The Blue boy stood by the Green boy for a few minutes. Then he went to a tree and broke off a branch. The Green boy said, "Don't hit me with that branch," thinking that's what Blue was about to do.

Blue answered him. "I'm not going to hit you. The branch is to pry loose the rocks that are holding your leg."

Blue pried loose the rocks. He tore his blue shirt into long strips and tied the branch to Green's leg. Then he helped Green walk home.

When Green's father saw his son's leg tied with the blue cloth, he cursed his boy. "I don't care if you were injured," he screamed. "You should have not let a Blue touch you."

Though Green knew his father was upset with him, he could not forget the Blue who had helped him. When his leg healed, he went into Blue Land to find his helper.

For a whole day Green walked in the neighborhoods of Blue Land. It took a lot of courage to do this because everywhere he went people slammed doors on him and called him names. Some young children even threw rocks at him. Finally, he found the boy who had helped him. He did not slam his door on Green. He welcomed him in his home.

Green was happy to see Blue, but he was surprised to see that his helper had clothes that combined the colors of blue and green.

"I thought you learned that green was bad. Why are you wearing green with your blue?" asked Green.

"Do you remember when I helped you when you were hurt? I tore up my blue shirt to make a splint for your leg. I figured that you became part of me, and I became part of you. In helping you and talking with you, I came to see that green is as good as blue."

"Won't the other Blues throw rocks at you when they find out you're a 'Green-lover?' " asked Green.

"I don't care what people think," said Blue. "It is right to help people whether they are blue or green."

The two boys became close friends. They often visited each other. They made up a new song which they taught to the children. It had these words:

> "Green is good, but so is Blue,
> Purple, Yellow and Red too —
> All the children should be glad;
> There is no color that is bad."

Little by little more Blues and Greens started visiting each other. Then they began going to each other's schools and churches. They even went beyond their own lands and visited the Yellows, Reds and Purples. After a while most people didn't call themselves "Greens" or "Blues" but simply "Rainbow People." And to this day their children sing, "There is no color that is bad."

LaBerge Maren

Chore's Magic

HE WAS GIVEN the name "Matthew" at birth. But since the time he could walk he was called "Chore." This was due to the fact that his mother and older sister made him do all the family's housework. Besides washing windows, scrubbing floors, mowing the lawn and emptying the garbage, he did dishes after every meal and snacks. Chore never had time for comic books, T.V. or any games played by children.

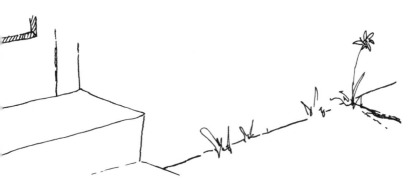

Chore's sister was Honeydew. She did nothing but sit around all day eating candy and reading movie magazines. When Honeydew would hit Chore for no good reason, their mother would say something like, "Careful, my precious daughter, that you don't hurt your hand on your stupid brother."

There was definitely something wrong with Chore's mother and sister.

As Honeydew grew up she followed her mother's example of being nasty to Chore. She called him names like "frogface" or "toad" when she got tired of "stupid" or "nitwit." She purposely and rudely pulled the stuffing out of his koala bear which he loved like a pet.

Though he was treated badly by his mother and sister, Chore loved them both. They were still all he had in the world since his father died when he was a baby. When they were unfair to him he made up excuses such as: "they must not be feeling well today." Once when Honeydew kicked him he said, "I hope you didn't hurt your foot." He was always nice.

One night after dinner Chore's mother and sister sent him out to buy five pounds of gumdrops. Both ate a lot of candy despite the warnings given them by their doctor and dentist. As he left home with the money, his mother warned, "Don't you open the pack of candy before you get home."

Chore did as he was told and bought the five pounds of gumdrops. As he came out of the candystore an old man dressed in rags asked him for a handout. Chore thought about how mad his mother would be if he opened the package of candy. But the man was hungry, maybe even starving. He gave the old man the whole five pounds of candy.

As the beggar took the gumdrops, an unusual thing happened. A person dressed in a blinding light appeared to Chore. He could not tell if it was a man or woman because the light was so bright.

22

Somewhat frightened, Chore asked, "Who are you?"

"That's not important," answered the person dressed in light. "You did a very nice thing for the beggar. As a reward I'm giving you two presents, one for your hands and one for your heart."

With that, the mysterious person put twenty pounds of gumdrops in the boy's hands. Chore was puzzled about the other reward. What could this present for his heart be?

Chore gave all the candy to his mother and sister. He told them about the beggar and the person dressed in light. Angered, his mother immediately called the candy store to see if they were missing twenty pounds of gumdrops.

After checking all of his supplies, the candyman told Chore's mother he was not missing any. He confirmed the story of the beggar who waited outside of his store. But he knew nothing about a mysterious person dressed in light.

The next day Chore's mother sent Honeydew to the same store for candy. She told her daughter to do the same thing as her brother — buy five pounds of gumdrops and give them to the beggar. She wasn't teaching her daughter to be generous. She wanted the reward of twenty more pounds. If it happened for Chore, it would happen for Honeydew. This was how she reasoned.

After arriving at the store Honeydew saw the same old beggar. After she bought her five pounds of gumdrops, she stopped to stare at the man in rags. She didn't want to give the man the whole five pounds. She hesitated, then finally threw the bag of candy at his feet.

As the beggar picked up the candy, the person dressed in light appeared. Without any exchange of words Honeydew was given a twenty pound bag.

"I knew I could get as much as my ignorant brother," she boasted as she ran home to mother with the goodies.

Once home, Honeydew and her mother reached into the

bag and greedily stuffed their faces. Crunch! Crackle! They were given chocolate-covered rocks. They almost broke their teeth.

Mother and Honeydew cursed Chore and kicked him. Quietly he went to his room.

Alone in his room, the person dressed in light appeared to him.

"Tell me who are you. How did you do the tricks with gumdrops and chocolate-covered rocks?" asked Chore.

"I'm just a person dressed in light. My tricks weren't that great. But I do have some magic to teach you."

"Will I be able to pull rabbits from a hat?" asked Chore excitedly.

"No, the magic I know has nothing to do with tricks. But it will work on your mother and sister."

In saying this the person dressed in light handed Chore a piece of paper and disappeared.

Chore read the paper the person had left him. It said:

> "Don't ever feel that you're weak
> Because you turn the other cheek.
> Seek not revenge when you're done dirt.
> Just give away your favorite shirt.
> If you're asked to walk a mile,
> Sprint for two in gracious style.
> Pray for those who give you chores,
> And heaven's magic will be yours."

Chore had just finished reading the message when there was a knock on his door. He opened his door and there were his mother and sister. He expected to be cursed and hit again. But instead they kissed him and said, "We're sorry, Matthew."

Chore tucked his secret message in the pocket by his heart. He had a feeling his magic was working.

La Berge Muren

26

Jonah

ERB AND HARVEY were twin brothers and twin brats. As eighth graders of Public School #13, they had a reputation for being bullies. They started fights at recess and broke things belonging to the school when the teachers weren't looking. They always picked on children younger and weaker than themselves.

One day, the twin brats did some damage to a new ten-speed bicycle belonging to Jonah, a seventh grader. They carved their names on the frame, kicked in its spokes and bent its wheels.

When Jonah saw his wrecked bike, he knew who had done the damage. He wanted to cry, but he held back his tears. He had saved up money for six months from his paper route to buy the bicycle, which was now a mess.

As Jonah walked his bike home from school, all he could think of was how to get even with Herb and Harvey. He wanted to fight both of them, even though they were bigger and older. He wanted to punish them badly, even if it meant getting hurt.

When Jonah arrived home, he was greeted by his Uncle Larry, who was visiting from out of town. He told his uncle about the twin brats and what they did to his bicycle. He told his uncle about his plan of fighting the two.

The uncle listened politely, and gave Jonah some advice.

"Jonah, I don't blame you for feeling very angry. I'll make sure your bike is fixed. It won't do any good to fight the two. Even if you won the fight, that wouldn't be the end of trouble. You might get even with them, but they would think of a new way to do something else to you or your bike. Let's settle this thing the right way. I'll take you to their parents' house. We'll talk to them."

Jonah was angry with his uncle. He didn't like his advice. He didn't want to talk to the twins or their parents. He wanted to settle everything with a fight.

The next morning Jonah got up as usual at five. As he was folding his newspapers all he could think of was Herb and Harvey with black eyes and bloody noses.

Uncle Larry drove Jonah along his paper route. As they were riding down Ross Avenue, Jonah pointed out to his uncle the home of Herb and Harvey. His uncle stopped the car.

"Keep going, Uncle. I don't deliver to Herb and Harvey. If I did, I would throw a newspaper through their window."

"I'm going to talk to their parents," answered his uncle. "Do you want to come with me?"

"No," answered Jonah. "I might say the wrong thing." He stayed in the car as the uncle went to the twins' house.

The twins' mother answered the door. She didn't look too happy about being awakened at 5:30 am. Uncle Larry gave her the facts about her sons: how they almost destroyed a two hundred dollar bicycle. The woman listened in silence. Then she asked, "How much are the damages.?"

"I think fifty dollars should handle it. I'll send you the bill from the bike shop," answered Jonah's uncle.

"I'm sorry this happened. My boys will pay for the damages. I will tell them that they must learn not to destroy what belongs to others."

When Jonah went to school that day, he tried to stay away from the twins. But they kept following him and trying to talk to him. Finally, he said, "Ok, what do you want?"

"We, we, aa just wa want to say we're sorry," stuttered the once-terrible twins.

"Wow!" answered Jonah. "Your mom must have given you some kind of a lecture. But I'm not accepting your apology. You guys better keep an eye on your bikes. You might just find your wheels kicked in."

Jonah walked away from the twins feeling good about himself. Now it was his turn to play the tough guy. He loved giving Herb and Harvey a taste of their own medicine.

That evening, Jonah told his uncle about what happened at school, and how he didn't accept the twins' apology.

Uncle Larry put his arm around Jonah and gave him some advice.

"Jonah, it took guts for Herb and Harvey to apologize. They act like bullies, but they're not really tough. Most bullies aren't. Why don't you be big and accept their apology? They're paying for their mistake. If you treat them like human beings, they may start acting like human beings."

Jonah thought about his uncle's advice. He didn't like the idea of apologizing.

"I can't do it," he told his uncle. "I hate those guys."

"Do you just want to be a small-minded person all your life, Jonah?"

Jonah didn't like that last remark. He didn't want to appear small-minded to his uncle. He phoned the twins and accepted their apology.

In the days that followed, Jonah and the twins didn't become close friends, but they did say "hello"; and they did learn to respect each other's property.

LaBerge Muren

Stumblefoot's Gift

STUMBLEFOOT WAS A little Alpine goat who always appeared to be off balance. His feet always seemed to touch ground at different times when he walked or ran.

Meg was Stumblefoot's master. She was a shepherd nomad who lived with her parents in the hill country of Palestine. Meg and Stumblefoot led carefree, happy lives and moved with the flocks wherever the grass was plentiful.

Meg and Stumblefoot had a favorite game they played together. Meg called the game "catch me if you can." It was a combination of tag, hide-and-seek, and dodge-ball. As soon as they were finished, Meg would give her goat a treat of wild roses. Stumblefoot loved wildflowers, like most children love ice cream.

It happened one morning that Meg could not find her goat.

"He's just playing our game," she thought. But after calling him for an hour with no luck, she realized he was lost. Meg asked her father and mother if they have seen him.

"Perhaps he's with your brothers," suggested her mother.

"You know he's a wanderer," reminded her father.

Meg checked with her brothers. They, too, guessed that he was out wandering. Meg fought to hold back her tears, fearing that she had lost her Stumblefoot.

"Just go out and look for him," suggested her brothers.

So, with her parents' permission, Meg set out to find her wandering friend.

After walking and calling all day, Meg realized it was too late to start back to her family tent. Not being afraid of the dark, she decided to spend the night in the open and return home at daybreak. Luckily, she found a cave carved in a hillside for shelter.

"This is a nice place to sleep," she thought as she gathered some dry grass for her bed.

Meg was about to fall asleep, when two people came into the cave. She saw faces of a man and woman. She lay still. As the man and woman drew closer, she heard a familiar sound. It was Stumblefoot!

"You crazy-legged creature!" shouted Meg. "I've been looking all over for you."

Meg hugged her pet, forgetting the man and woman who stood before her.

"My name is Joseph," said the man. "This is my wife, Mary. Your goat followed us up this hill. I hope you don't mind sharing this cave. There wasn't room for us in town."

Meg welcomed Mary and Joseph. She was used to sharing everything she had. She helped her new friends gather dry grass for their beds.

Exhausted, Meg fell asleep next to Stumblefoot. After a few hours, when she was in her deepest sleep, she was suddenly awakened by familiar voices.

"Meg, it's me. Wake up."

Meg realized she wasn't in a dream. It was her mother calling. Her father and brothers were outside the cave. There were other people there also.

"Look at the baby, Meg. Isn't he beautiful!"

Meg rubbed her eyes. It was her mother speaking. Her mother was holding a baby. She had seen animals born in the wild, but being the last of her mother's children, she had never seen a baby.

"Mom, what's happening? I know I'm not dreaming. Whose baby is that? How did you get here?"

"We were looking for you, Meg, when some neighboring shepherds brought us here to see the newborn child, Jesus."

For the next few days Meg's family tended their sheep near the cave of Jesus' birth. When Meg played her game with Stumblefoot, he often hid in the cave. When Meg found him, she would say to Mary, "Stumblefoot must love Jesus. He always comes here to hide from me. I wish your baby was old enough to play with us."

"That's a nice thought," said Mary. "Maybe some day you can visit us at our home in Nazareth. Then all of you can play."

"You don't live around here?" asked Meg somewhat disappointed.

"No, we just came here for the census," explained Mary.

The next few years passed quickly for Meg. When she wasn't helping her family tend the sheep, she was playing her game with Stumblefoot.

One year, Meg and her family had to travel some distance to find better grass for their flock. As they overlooked the village of Nazareth, Meg remembered the invitation of Mary. Going from house to house, Meg finally found her friends from the cave. Jesus was four, old enough to play the game of "catch me if you can." Meg, Stumblefoot and Jesus played for hours.

After a few weeks in Nazareth, Meg's family had to move on. It was hard for Meg to leave Jesus, but she had to go with her family.

Years later, after Stumblefoot had died and Meg had a family of her own, she heard more about Jesus. Some people who were called Jesus' "disciples" told her many stories. They told her about the time he preached at Nazareth and how the townspeople tried to throw him down a hillside. They told her how other people threw rocks at him after he cured a man on the Sabbath.

"You mean people tried to hurt him, and he got away from them?" asked Meg.

"Yes", they replied. "He was good at dodging rocks and hiding from his enemies. Our Master told us once that he learned to dodge and hide from a game he played with a little girl and her goat."

Meg smiled with deep satisfaction. She had almost forgotten her goat and their game.

Then the disciples went on to tell Meg more about Jesus.

"There came a time when Jesus could no longer dodge the rocks or the people who wanted to hurt him. Soldiers arrested him, and he was put to death."

At this point of the story, Meg felt very sad and began to cry.

"Don't cry, Meg," continued the disciples."The story doesn't end there. Jesus did die. But he only stayed in the grave for a few days. He came out alive. He lives now and forever. So will you if you believe in him. You see, evil people never really caught him. Neither did death."

As Meg reached old age, she felt herself becoming weaker until the day came when it was her time to leave the world. One day she closed her eyes, just as she had done many years ago in the cave on the Bethlehem hillside. Death took her gently, as though she was in a deep sleep. Then suddenly she was awakened with a gentle light. She saw her parents, her brothers, Stumblefoot and Jesus with Mary and Joseph.

Meg realized she wasn't in a dream. It was like the first Christmas night all over again.

"Thank you for Heaven," said Meg.

"Thank you for your gift," answered Jesus.

When a heavenly question mark appeared on Meg's face, Jesus explained: "Thanks for Stumblefoot and your game."

Sticks and stones may break my bones but names will never hurt me.

LaBerge Muren

B. B. Wolf

ONCE THERE WERE three pigs named Sticks, Stones, and Breakmybones. They were brothers. Such unusual names were reminders of their family motto: "Sticks and stones may break my bones but names will never hurt me."

When the three became adults, they said to their parents, "Mom and dad, we are going to the middle of the forest to build a home, a restaurant and a spaghetti factory. We will work hard, save our money and even build a home for you."

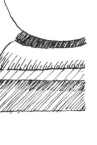

Their parents were pleased, but they warned their sons of the evil forest outlaw, Bigbad Wolf.

The sons appreciated the warning. They kissed their parents goodbye and began their journey to the middle of the forest.

While traveling, they discussed their plans.

"I'll design the spaghetti factory," said Sticks.

"I'll design the restaurant," said Stones.

"And I'll design our home," said Breakmybones. "But we must agree on one thing. We shall always work together and never give Bigbad a chance to attack any one of us."

The brothers agreed with Breakmybones. They knew that Bigbad was only brave when he could pick on someone weaker than himself.

When the brothers reached the middle of the forest, they gathered sticks for the spaghetti factory, straw for the restaurant and stones for their home. They began to work together. From a distance, Bigbad watched and prepared his menu: bacon for breakfast, ham for lunch and pork chops for dinner.

After much hard work, the brothers finished their three buildings. They invited a few neighbors to the grand opening of the restaurant and factory. But before the invitations were even in the mail, Bigbad decided to make his move against the brothers. Thinking that a pig would be in each of the three buildings, he huffed and puffed and blew down the spaghetti factory and the restaurant. None of the three pigs were inside. Bigbad was furious.

"They tricked me by staying together," he shouted. "I'll take them all three at a time."

The Wolf went to the stone home of the pigs and began calling them names like "stinking sissies." Little did he realize that the brothers did not lose their heads over name-calling. The brothers stayed inside their home.

Bigbad huffed and puffed and couldn't blow down their house. The brothers said from a window: "Sticks and straw were blown away, but stones are here to stay."

The brothers discussed what they would do if Bigbad decided to come down the chimney. Sticks suggested putting a pot of boiling water in the fireplace. Stones thought it was a good idea.

"We can put 'spaghetti with wolf sauce' on our menu when we rebuild our restaurant," said Stones.

Breakmybones was not happy with his brothers' suggestions. "Let's not be silly," he warned his brothers. "Remember that our parents taught us some important rules. If we are mean to someone, he will be mean to someone else."

"How would you handle the problem?" asked Stones.

"We'll let him come down the chimney," said Breakmybones, "and as soon as he's in the fireplace, we'll invite him to dinner. Who would not prefer homemade spaghetti to raw pork chops?"

The brothers agreed with Breakmybones. When Bigbad came down the chimney, they made their offer. Although he was surprised by the invitation, Bigbad accepted. He loved the spaghetti. He asked for seconds and thirds. Then he asked the brothers to teach him how to cook like them.

"We'll teach you to cook after you help us rebuild our factory and restaurant," said the brothers. "We have to make sure you are sincere and not up to your old tricks."

So B. B. Wolf helped the brothers rebuild. Little by little he earned trust. There were a few times when he went back to his old ways of threatening to get attention, but he quickly came to his senses after a good meal.

Even today travelers to the middle of the forest can stop at the "Three Pigs Plus One Family Restaurant" and see an old wolf flipping pancakes and pizzas. His chef's hat carries the initial "B. B." which no longer means "Big Bad", but rather "Best Baker."

LaBerge Muren

An Angel
for
Mary Jane

THERE IS LIVING TODAY a most unusual being. She may be hundreds of thousands of years old. Her exact age is a secret, but she is forever young despite her years. Her name is Colga. She is one of those angels who remained faithful when Lucifer went on his "power trip" wanting to be God.

Ages ago, God said to Colga, "I want you to join me in a great but dangerous adventure. As you know, I have Earth prepared with many plants and animals. It's time now for the best part to come alive — people. The first two, Adam and Eve, are ready to awaken. But before I bring light to their eyes, I will send them invisible guardians from here. You are chosen for this pilot mission, Colga. Are you willing?"

"I'll take good care of Adam and Eve," Colga promised. She was pleased with her new assignment.

"I must remind you that Adam and Eve will be difficult," warned God. "Our one-time friend, Lucifer, prowls around Earth these days. You know what a troublemaker he is."

Colga felt able to handle her assignment. She had been given the assignment of guarding the first parents of the planet Alphon which was in a different galaxy from Earth's. She had no problem with them or any other Alphons.

Shortly after she arrived for her mission with Earth's first parents, Colga saw Adam and Eve listening to the tall tales of Lucifer. The bad angel's pitch was: "Don't be satisfied with second best. You can be like God. Rebel at once and demand equality."

"He's a liar, don't believe him," shouted Colga. But Adam and Eve did not listen to her inspirations. They took the wrong advice and began to choose greed over sharing and hate over love. As a result, they made misery for themselves.

Colga reported back to God. "I blew my assignment," she moaned. If angels could cry, heaven would have had a downpour.

God was not angry with Colga. "You did your best," he assured her. "This was a tough assignment. Earthlings are not like the Alphons who had no radical freedom. Adam and Eve have a special ingredient called "free will" or "heart." If they are not careful in monitoring this special ingredient, greed may look better than sharing and hate more appealing than love."

"Can't I stop them from making the wrong choices?" asked Colga.

"You and I can help them recognize the beauty in love and the happiness brought by sharing. But we can't force them, Colga. Unlike the Alphons, they share our kind of life. They are free."

"How can I help humans like Adam and Eve? They're free, but they take the wrong advice." Colga was plainly confused.

"To help humans you must use your imagination," said God. "Up to this time you have not had much use for your power to dream new ideas. Now you must put it to full use."

As more people were born on Earth, Colga was given other assignments. Little by little she began to use her imagination. She helped Noah with ideas for his Ark. She inspired the woman who saved the life of Moses by floating him on the river in a basket. For thousands of years she had success with the people she was given to help, protect and inspire. Most of them chose sharing over greed and love over hate.

After many thousands of years of service as a guardian angel, Colga asked for a vacation.

"Do you think I could spend some time on Alphon?" Colga asked God. "I need a break from Earth and a chance to visit with my Alphon friends."

"All right," said God. "I see you need a change of pace. But before you go, I have one more assignment for you — a teenager in the United States of America. Her name is Mary Jane."

"A teenager?" asked a surprised Colga. "I thought we were always assigned babies."

"That's normally true. But Mary Jane's angel needed a rest more than you. He just couldn't cope any further."

"What's Mary Jane's problem?" asked Colga. "Does she choose greed over sharing and hate over love?"

"It's not that simple," answered God. "She doesn't seem to choose at all. She just sits in a field and eats the purple clover."

"The purple clover?" asked Colga.

"Yes. She eats this plant which lessens her heart's power to choose. She is turning into a robot. She's more like an Alphon than a human at present."

Colga went immediately to her new assignment. She tried to get Mary Jane interested in sports, but the girl showed no response. She tried to get Mary Jane interested in reading. This, too, was rejected. She tried to get her interested in her family, and the beauty of human relationships. Everything failed. All Mary Jane wanted to do was eat the purple clover.

For the first time in centuries, Colga was angry when she reported back to God.

"Mary Jane does not respond to anything I suggest. I give up! I want my vacation now! Someone else will have to work on the purple clover girl."

God looked straight into the fiery eyes of his angel and said, "Not yet, Colga. I gave you a great imagination. You haven't begun to use it. Go back to Mary Jane, and for the first time in your life use your imagination."

Colga went back to Earth, determined to try harder. She found Mary Jane, as usual, sitting in a field of the purple clover. She sat beside her and turned on her angelic imagination. Then, seeing a cow in a nearby meadow, Colga bolted like lightning to the side of the animal. She lifted the cow, as only an angel can do, and plopped it next to Mary Jane.

"Eat," commanded Colga. The cow began to eat the purple clover.

When Mary Jane saw what was happening, she tried to be angry. But she couldn't really feel anger or hate or love. She had to watch without interest as the invader ate all her purple clover.

After a few days of not having any more purple clover, Mary Jane went home. Within a few weeks she started to feel healthy. She ate regular foods like carrots and hamburgers. But most importantly, she began to experience "heart," the ability to feel emotions and make choices. At first she was hateful as when she purposely messed up the kitchen. Then she began to help and share. She helped her sister wash the dishes.

Seeing that her mission was accomplished, Colga reported back to God. She was given her relaxation time on the planet Alphon. But to heaven's surprise, she came back early from her vacation.

"I didn't realize how dull the Alphons were until I met humans," she confessed to God. "Adam and Eve and Mary Jane are well worth the trouble they cause... My next assignment, please!"

LaBerge Muren

Lucky Lady

S OME SAID SHE was a hundred years old. Others said she was two hundred. Thin and worn, she maintained her proud Roman face — something age could not take away from her. Almost everyone loved her. Rich and poor wanted to hold her. Lucky Lady was her name. She was a silver coin.

This little coin with the face of the Emperor Caesar had many masters in her lifetime. Her present master was a soldier, a gambler, who never felt guilty in taking a man's last dime.

The soldier was Kevin, an unusual name for one serving the Roman Emperor. He came from Ireland, a land far from Rome. He had joined the Roman Army for adventure. Next to traveling, Kevin loved gambling best of all life's pleasures. He loved Lucky Lady. He talked to her, and honestly believed that she helped him win most of his bets. She was his partner, his lucky coin.

Kevin and Lucky Lady traveled through most of the countries which surround the Mediterranean Sea. It happened that while they were in Palestine, Kevin caught a disease which wouldn't go away. It was called leprosy. The people who contracted this disease seemed to just rot away, like trees fallen in the forest. Since it was thought to be contageous, the authorities made the lepers live beyond the city limits in the wilderness.

Kevin had lived in the wilderness for about a year before he had even come close to a healthy person. Then one day a man came up to him. The man had companions, and they called him "rabbi" or "teacher." At first Kevin thought the teacher was a robber. So he held tightly to Lucky Lady.

"Don't worry, Soldier," said one of the teacher's men. "We don't want your money."

Kevin was surprised by the honesty of these people who had dared to come so close to one with a contageous disease. He asked the teacher, "What do you want from me? I am a leper."

"Let the teacher help you," said one of the men.

At that moment the teacher put his hand on Kevin's face. And as he did so he asked the question, "Do you want to be cured?"

Being a gambling man and feeling he had nothing to lose, Kevin replied, "Yes, I want to be cured." He said this not really believing it could happen.

For the moment that the teacher held his hand on Kevin's

forehead, he felt as though he were transported to another world.

"What kind of a man is this?" he thought to himself. "Is he really healing me?"

The teacher took his hand away from Kevin. The leprosy was gone.

Kevin touched his skin. He fell on his knees to thank the man who had cured him. He was not used to falling on his knees or thanking anyone. He was a tough and self-reliant soldier. But now he was crying like a baby, thanking this stranger who had miraculous power to heal. His body had new flesh. But more importantly his soul, the spirit inside of him, was cleared up. He experienced love for the man who cured him.

"What can I do for you, teacher?" asked Kevin.

"Just take your coin," answered the teacher, "and give it as an offering to the poor in thanksgiving for your cure."

Kevin did as the teacher suggested. He gave his Lucky Lady to a religious leader, a Pharisee, whose job it was to help the poor.

It happened by chance that the teacher and the Pharisee met one day. The Pharisee had been upset with the way the teacher called God his Father. The Pharisee was jealous of the teacher and wanted to put him to shame in front of the people who loved the teacher. To do this, he thought up a trick question. He asked the teacher in front of the people: "Should a Jew pay taxes to the Roman Caesar?" If the teacher were to answer "yes," then he would be recognized as unpatriotic. If he said "no," then he could be reported to the Roman authorities and be put in jail.

The teacher didn't fall into the Pharisee's trap. He didn't answer "yes" or "no." Instead, he asked the Pharisee if he had a coin. The Pharisee reached into his pocket and pulled out Lucky Lady. The teacher asked the Pharisee to look at the coin. Then he asked him a question.

"Whose picture is on the coin?"

The Pharisee looked at Lucky Lady and recognized the proud face of Caesar.

"It is the face of Caesar," he answered somewhat annoyed with the question.

There was a moment of silence as the people looked at the teacher. Then he spoke.

"Give to Caesar the things that are Caesar's and to God the things that are God's."

The people applauded the teacher's answer. The Pharisee knew he had been outsmarted. In his anger he threw Lucky Lady as far as he could.

The old coin felt good as she sailed through the air and landed between two rocks. At last she was free from the hands of a greedy man. She could rest where no one would disturb her.

Years passed and Lucky Lady remained between the rocks. The rains had given her a nice coat of moss and the winds had covered her with a blanket of sand. One day, a hand touched her. It was a familiar hand, that of the soldier named Kevin.

"Lucky Lady, it is you!" exclaimed Kevin. "I have a lot to tell you. Remember the teacher who cured me? Remember how he outsmarted the Pharisee who threw you between the rocks? That teacher was the Son of God. He was raised from the dead and his followers celebrate their belief in him every Sunday. I want you to help in that celebration."

Lucky Lady was happy for Kevin. She didn't mind it at all when the ex-soldier melted her along with other coins to make a beautiful chalice for the celebration of the Lord's Supper.

The people who saw Kevin's chalice marveled at its beauty, especially at the sacred time when it heard the Teacher's words: "This is my blood." It actually turned pink.

Some said it was miraculous. Others said the pink was just in the imagination . Only Kevin knew for sure. He knew the pinkness was his Lucky Lady blushing for joy at being able to give herself to God.

LaBerge Muren

Scotty's Dad

WHILE MOST BABIES were throwing food from their high chairs, Scotty Smith was throwing a football. When little ones were learning to walk, he was already running laps. When preschoolers were memorizing their A-B-C's, he was spelling words like ''score'' and ''touchdown.''

When Mrs. Smith was asked why Scotty did adult exercises as a child, she answered: "Scotty wasn't born into our family. He was recruited by his father to play football." No one criticized Scotty's Dad because he only allowed Scotty to have barbells and other athletic equipment when other boys his age were playing with trucks and stuffed animals. They knew pro football players could become famous and rich. And they wanted to share the glory (and money).

A family doctor warned Mr. Smith about overdeveloping Scotty. A psychiatrist told him he was just reliving his own frustrated dreams in Scotty and that it was bad for the boy. But Mr. Smith was determined to raise his son his own way.

From the time he could walk, Scotty went daily to the park with his father to learn the fundamentals of blocking, tackling, running, passing and catching. Whenever Scotty did poorly he was yelled at. When he did well, he was rewarded with ice cream. By the time he was five years old he was playing with the ten year olds. This was against league rules, but the authorities made an exception for Scotty at the insistence of his father.

Scotty's team was the Bulldogs. He was their captain. During his first season the Bulldogs won all their games. Scotty's running and passing were so sensational that he was written up in the newspaper as "Sensational Scotty Scattback."

With an undefeated record for the season, Scotty's team was to play for the State championship. The Wildcats were the opponents. Scotty's Bulldogs were favored by six points.

Before the championship game, Scotty's coach, Harold Hittem, took the team to church. Scotty, who liked to talk to God, made this prayer:

"Dear God, thank you for all the games we won this year. Thank you for mommy. Thank you for daddy. But don't let him swear at me during the game. Amen."

Now it was time for the game. The stadium was packed to capacity. The Bulldogs were confident of victory — especially after going to church. The Wildcats didn't go to church. The Bulldogs felt confident that God was on their side.

The Wildcats kicked off. A high end-over-end football landed in Scotty's arms. Bulldog fans yelled: "Run it all the way, Scotty." During the regular season Scotty had often taken the opening kickoff for a touchdown.

Whomp! A Wildcat hit Scotty as soon as he caught the ball. He fumbled. The Wildcats picked up the ball and scored. The whole game went like this. Every time Scotty touched the football, a Wildcat would make him fumble. Needless to say, Scotty's team lost 72 to 0.

After the game, Scotty rushed out of the locker room without even taking a shower. He did not want to see his dad. He knew his dad would be angry. But he didn't know how his dad would react, because he had never lost before.

"I wonder if he'll hit me," thought Scotty. It didn't matter. Since he was hit so often in the game, one more blow wouldn't matter.

Scotty took a secret way to his home. He went through the field which had the big fences and "no trespassing" signs posted. He wanted to be by himself.

As he walked through the field, he talked to God.

"God, I thought you listen to and help those who believe in you. I went to church with my team. The Wildcats didn't go to church. We prayed and lost. They didn't pray and won. How do you explain that?"

As Scotty was talking to God, he heard a cry.

"Help! Someone please help me!"

Scotty looked around and didn't see anyone. He heard the voice again. This time he saw where it was coming from — the old, abandoned well with the "danger" sign. He went up to the well and saw that a little girl had fallen in.

Scotty ran home as fast as he could. He called the fire department, and within a few minutes the firemen were at the well. The firemen quickly rescued the girl. Some newspaper photographers were there and took Scotty's picture for the paper. The girl's parents thanked him and promised to send him a reward.

Alone in his room that night, Scotty was still unhappy. He still hadn't seen his dad since the game. (His mother said his dad had to take care of some business). Again Scotty talked to God.

"God, I still want to know why you didn't listen to my prayer. How could we have lost 72 to O after we went to church? Now my dad probably won't speak to me for a week. How could you let this happen? My religion teacher tells me: 'ask from God and you shall receive.' Did you mix us up with the Wildcats? I know you have a lot of people to keep track of."

When Scotty finished asking God his questions, he heard a voice:

"My son, your prayers for victory weren't wasted. They went to help that little girl who had fallen in the well. If you had not lost the game, you would not have cut through the field. The little girl might still be in the well. Your prayers were heard, even though you didn't get exactly what you wanted."

At first, Scotty thought God had finally answered him. Then he realized the voice belonged to his dad. A smile came to Scotty's face. His dad wasn't angry. He understood. Scotty knew his prayer was really answered.

LaBerge Muren

Moneybags

HERE ONCE WAS a little boy who had more toys than all his preschool friends. He had so many little trucks that his dad had to build a special garage to house them. He had so many little ships that his dad built a special swimming pool for him to sail them. He had so many stuffed animals that his dad built an extra room on their house which was called the "zoo." The boy's name was Michael McCoon. But everyone called him "Moneybags."

When Moneybags was twenty years old he was still collecting toys. But with the years, his toys got bigger. Now he collected real cars, and his father was getting tired of building him garages.

"I wish Moneybags would go out and work for a living," said his father. But Moneybags didn't have to go out and work. He was spoiled rotten. He got everything he wanted because his parents had never said "no" to him.

When Moneybags was thirty years old his parents died and left him their vast fortune. But as he got older, he grew more and more unhappy, despite all his money. He found out that his money could not control the seasons. And, he was forever complaining about the heat or the cold.

One day, Moneybags decided to challenge the very elements of Nature. "I do not have to put up with the Four Seasons," he told Sam, his best friend and pilot of his private plane. "If it gets too cold in one place, I'll have you fly me where it is warmer, Sam. If it is too warm, I'll have you fly me where it is cool. With my planes and money, Mother Nature will have no say over me."

Sam looked at Moneybags as if to say, "You better not try to outsmart Mother Nature." But, out of respect for his boss, he didn't say anything.

For the next year strange things happened to Moneybags. When rain bothered him in Washington, he flew to California. When the smog stung his eyes, he went to Texas. But that was worse, because he ran into a hurricane. He went back to Washington because he decided rain wasn't so bad after all. But then there was something new in the atmosphere, ash from a volcano.

"I am determined to control nature," insisted Moneybags.

Sam knew his boss was making a mistake and he gave him some advice.

"Boss, he said, "there are laws we must respect. There are the laws of man, such as the speed limit. There are the laws of God, such as the ten Commandments. And there are the laws of Nature, such as 'summer brings heat.' If you don't respect these laws, things will go bad for you."

Moneybags didn't want anyone preaching to him, so he told Sam to mind his own business. But Sam didn't mind his own business and kept warning Moneybags. This cost Sam his job.

After firing Sam, Moneybags hired a certain Doctor Placebo to be his right-hand man. This so-called "doctor" did not have a medical degree. He once made a lot of pet foot called "Doctor's Delight", so everyone thought he was a veternarian, but actually, he was simply a scoundrel.

When Doctor Placebo found out Moneybags wanted control over Nature, he came to him for a deal.

"Moneybags, my friend, I can give you control over Mother Nature for a mere hundred dollars a day. I have invented a special drug called 'Fun Season Syrup.' If you take my drug every day, the weather will always be beautiful. You will never feel the pain of heat or chill."

Moneybags fell for the fake doctor's promise of happiness. Soon he was taking two hundred dollars a day worth of Fun Season Syrup — a mixture of prune juice and a drug used to put elephants to sleep when they are moved from the jungle to civilization. Moneybags soon lost a lot of weight, as well as money. The evil Doctor Placebo had taken over his life.

After being on the Fun Season drug for a year, Moneybags realized he had not been out of his room. Rain, heat, fog and even earthquakes had come and gone. But he was too drugged to notice any of them.

It happened that Moneybag's once faithful friend found out where he was being kept by Doctor Placebo. He went to visit him by night when Placebo was sleeping, for the evil syrup sorcerer allowed his captive no visitors.

"Moneybags, it's me, your old friend, Sam." The once richest man in the U.S.A. could barely open his eyes, but he did recognize his old friend.

"I'm going to take you out of here, Moneybags. This is no way to live. That mad doctor is ruining your health. You're just a skeleton of your former self."

Sam managed to take Moneybags out through a window. Having lost so much weight, he was easy to carry. He brought him to his own home where he gave him real medical care from a real doctor.

Moneybags didn't live too much longer after being rescued by Sam. But, at least he had the satisfaction of being able to get off the Fun Season Syrup and enjoy a few real days. Doctor Placebo was, of course, thrown in jail. And when the day came for Moneybags to die, his friend, Sam, was there at his bedside.

At Moneybags' grave, Sam wrote a verse for people to read.

"Here lies Moneybags McCoon.
He wasn't satisfied with the Moon.
He wanted power over Sky and Sun.
Of all the Seasons he wanted none.
Placebo said, 'I'll grant your wishes.
You'll be lord of beasts and fishes.
You will master Wind and Rain.
You will never suffer pain.'
Unfortunately, Placebo lied.
Moneybags prematurely died.
All you who read this verse,
Do not fall beneath his curse.
Take the Seasons as they come.
Each will have its pain and fun.
Little children, love the Snow.
Love the Rain so flowers grow.
Love July's scorching heat
As well as Fog with silent feet.

LaBerge Muren

The Frog Princess

ERIN WAS LUCKIER than most nine year olds. She had her very own castle.

"I love my castle," she told her Mom. "It's a lot nicer than Bertram's tree house which he never shares with me." (Bertram was Erin's ten-year old brother who only let boys enter his tree house).

"Where is your castle, my princess?" asked Erin's mother.

"It's by the river. What it really is, Mom, is a big rock with holes carved into it so it seems like it has windows and doors."

"Do be careful when you play by the river," cautioned Erin's mother. "I'm proud that you have a castle more beautiful than Bertram's tree house. Say 'hi' to the king and queen when you see them." (Erin's mother loved fantasy as much as Erin).

One afternoon after she did her homework, Erin went to her castle. It was here that she composed all the little songs she sang to her mother. Today she would sing about her brother. She tried thinking of words to rhyme with stingy, but could think of none. Then she thought of "icky," the perfect word for her brother.

"Melted candy can be sticky;
Mathematics can be tricky;
But you, Bertram, are just icky..."

As Erin was singing her song, a frog jumped out of the river, climbed the rock and sat next to her.

"Hello, little girl," said the frog. "Mind if I sit next to you?"

Erin jumped so suddenly when she heard a human voice coming from a frog that she almost fell down the stairway of her castle. Something inside her said 'run,' but she was frozen from a mixture of fear and curiosity.

"Did you speak, Mr. Frog?"

"Now don't be afraid. Yes, I did speak. I won't hurt you."

With some pinkness returning to her whitened face, Erin asked the frog if he was the one in the storybook.

"Are you the prince who was enchanted by a witch and had to live in a frog until the spell was broken by a kiss?"

"Now don't you worry, little girl. I am one hundred percent frog. I've never even seen a witch."

"Are you sure you're not a prince or someone like that?" Erin was still skeptical.

"Little girl," began the frog...

"You can call me Erin. My Mom calls me 'princess'."

"Erin," continued the frog, "I am not a prince or any other kind of human being. I just happen to be able to talk. And I'm talking to you because I'm bored. You would find your life very dull if all you did was catch flies, swim and hide from fish and fishermen. I wonder what it would be like to paint pictures, build skyscrapers, make medicines, fight wars and travel to the moon. My life seems so limited. I would do anything to be a person. But to tell the truth, I don't really know what it means to be a person."

Erin was amazed by how much the frog knew about people.

"My Mom says that 'being a person' means being willing to say 'thank you' or 'I'm sorry' at the proper times. She says it means being able to enjoy rain and rainbows, fish and frogs. But most of all, it means loving those who are mean to you. She told me this last part after Bertram hit me."

"Who's Bertram?" asked the frog with anger in his voice. "Why would anyone try to hurt you?"

"Oh, Bertram's just my brother. He's older, and he has this tree house which only boys can enter. He thinks little sisters have a place far away from older brothers. I don't think he wants to hurt me. But when he slaps me, it does sting."

"Does Bertram hate you?" asked the frog.

At the mention of 'hate,' Erin began to cry. She didn't want to think of her brother hating her, but in her heart she felt he did hate her.

"I want to be his friend," cried Erin. "But he always says, 'little sisters can't be friends.' "

The frog saw that the more questions he asked, the sadder Erin became. So he decided to change the subject.

"Let me teach you some tricks," said the frog. "I used to be a boy's pet. He trained me for frog jumping contests. I can even do sommersaults."

The frog proceeded to do sommersaults along with a few front flips. For the moment, Erin forgot about Bertram and sang a little song while watching the frog.

"Earthquakes and Bertram have their faults;
Banks and jumpers have their vaults;
And this talking frog does sommersaults!"

"More! More!" Erin shouted as the frog finished his act.

"That's enough for today," he answered. "I'm a little tired. There's always tomorrow."

"Will you come back tomorrow?" asked Erin. "Please come back to my castle. You can make me laugh and I will sing for you." The frog agreed.

The next day Erin came back to her castle. But she was an unhappy princess with tears in her eyes.

"What's wrong?" asked the frog. "Why the tears? Why no little homespun songs?"

"It's my brother again. I tried to climb into his tree house to tell him about you, and he tore my dress."

The frog was puzzled by the complication of human problems. He wondered if all brothers and sisters hated each other. Frogs, he thought, were lucky. They didn't have any problem in sharing the river. Finally, he spoke.

"I'll make you laugh again, Erin." Saying this, he began his acrobatics. He did flips and sommersaults. Still she did not smile. He did a double sommersault — something he had never done before. Still she didn't smile. Not knowing what to do next, he went to his friend, the venerable old bullfrog.

72

"Venerable, old one," he asked. "How can I make a child laugh?"

"Croaaaaak" came the answer, which translated meant: "Don't just entertain the child. She has her T.V. for that. Have her run through the mud with you."

The talking frog just stood there before the venerable old bullfrog and wondered if he had heard correctly. He didn't want to be disrespectful, but he thought the idea of running through the mud was silly. Nevertheless, he obeyed...

After taking Erin for a run through the mud, the talking frog realized she was smiling again. Before he knew it, she was singing a new song:

"It's lots of fun to be all wet;
This is the muddiest I've been yet —
Can I tame you to be my pet?"

The frog was flattered by the last words of Erin's song. It was a question she wanted answered.

"Can a frog be the pet of a human?" he asked himself. In his confusion, the frog went back to the old bullfrog for more advice.

"Venerable old and wise one. can I, a miserable frog, be a pet to Erin?"

"Croaaak," came the answer, a word which looks meaningless in written form but has meaning only to the ears of frogs. This "croaaak" translated to "Tell Erin she is to be your pet. You are to tame her at the river."

If the talking frog was confused before, now he was in a state of shock. Putting aside his own feelings, he told Erin of the old bullfrog's advice.

"Erin, I can't be your pet. But you can be mime."

Erin laughed at the idea of being a frog's pet, but she came to the river every day to play with him. She considered the frog a real friend.

While, at first, Erin didn't tell anyone about her friend, the talking frog, she finally wrote a story for her English teacher entitled, "My Friend, the Talking Frog." When her teacher gave her an "A" for imagination, Erin told her that it wasn't make-believe. She insisted her story was true. The teacher told Erin's Mother to take her to the psychologist for testing, and to the priest for confession.

Erin's mother looked the teacher in the eye and said, "My daughter isn't crazy, nor does she lie. She does have a very real castle by the river and a most unusual talking frog for a friend. She used to always fight with her brother. Now she is peaceful and forgiving. Who am I to say her froggy friend isn't real?"

La Berge Muren

Dog
Days

BERNIE HELPED PEOPLE, especially those who were lost in the snow. Every time he did a good deed like bringing a warm drink to one caught in a snowbank, he got rewarded with money. He wore a small bank around his neck so it was easy for people to drop in nickels, dimes, quarters, and even silver dollars. Because he helped so many people, Bernie was probably the richest St. Bernard dog in the world.

Actually, the money didn't belong to Bernie, but to his master. But it may as well have belonged to Bernie, for his master built him the largest dog house in the world. It was a block long and had twelve rooms, all nicely furnished with thick shag carpets.

Because Bernie was generous by nature, he decided to share his twelve room house with others. Some of the rooms he shared with relatives, and others with total strangers. All Bernie demanded of those staying in his house was that they keep their rooms clean. On the first day of every month he would visit all the rooms of his house, much like a landlord visits his tenants.

It happened that Bernie allowed a coyote, named Curly, to use one of his rooms. It was the first room the coyote ever had. He was used to sleeping out in the open. Curly loved his room, especially the thick shag rug. But he made many messes on his rug and never bothered to clean up.

When Bernie inspected Curly's room he was very upset over the messy condition. The rug was almost ruined. Curly just didn't care how he left his room. He was a slob.

"I don't think you can stay in my house any longer, Curly," said Bernie. "You haven't kept your promise to keep your room clean."

"Oh please, let me stay, kind landlord," begged Curly. "You can't send me out into the open fields again. Farmers shoot at coyotes. Food is hard to get. And I'll be forced to live with a bunch of crazies who howl under a full moon. Please don't send me back."

Bernie was a soft touch, so he decided to give Curly a second chance.

"I'll let you stay, but on the condition that you clean up this mess and take care of your room."

"I promise, I promise," said Curly, but under his breath he said, "Sucker."

Now it happened that Curly had allowed Sammy Squirrel to take over his old living quarters, a cave by the open fields. In order to live in the coyote's old home, Sammy had to gather nuts for Curly. This was his way of paying rent. Every month Curly would come by his old home and have his fill of nuts from what Sammy had gathered.

On the very same day that he was given a second chance by Bernie, Curly went to his old home to get his fill of nuts. To his shock there were only a few nuts, where generally he expected a feast of a few hundred. Sammy explained that he had been sick and that he had shared what nuts he had gathered with some elderly squirrels who could no longer climb trees. Curly did not like Sammy's excuses and said, "You little disguised rodent. How dare you not have a pile of nuts for my enjoyment. You can no longer stay in my cave. Get out!"

"But Mr. Coyote," begged Sammy, "please give me another chance. I will go out tomorrow and work doubly hard. I had many of my fellow squirrels to care for this last month. I'm sorry I was not able to meet your demands."

"Excuses! Excuses! How I hate a whiny, miserable, excuse-making long-tailed beggar like you. Get out now! If I catch you here, you are done for."

With these harsh words, Sammy Squirrel left the cave.

As he was walking along feeling sorry for himself, Sammy met Bernie, who asked him why he was so sad.

"You wouldn't understand," answered Sammy. "Curly just kicked me out of his cave. But he had a right to. I just couldn't gather enough nuts for him this month."

"Why that poor excuse for a prairie dog!" barked Bernie.

"Who does he think he is kicking you out? I just gave him a second chance to stay at my plush house. Why he doesn't even deserve a mongrel motel, let alone a mansion for thoroughbreds!"

Bernie was so angry that for the first time in his life he felt hot under his collar. He marched right to Curly's room and growled, "Curly, you're out! It was bad enough that you left your room a mess, but then you begged for mercy. I was kindhearted and gave you a second chance. Then you turned right around and threw Sammy Squirrel out into the cold."

"O please," begged Curly.

"Your time for 'O pleases' is over, Curly. You can go back to the fields. Your room is now turned over to Sammy, who is more deserving than you."

So that's what happened. Curly went back to dodging the farmer's bullets and howling under the moon with the other coyotes, while Sammy lived happily with his new friend Bernie.

LaBerge Muren

Paddedpants

TWO THOUSAND YEARS AGO before there were such things as monster movies or TV cartoons, there lived an eight-year old named Terry, who could tell stories about superheroes. Once when Terry was late in coming home from school, he told his mother that a dragon with a thousand tails and a million eyes had held him prisoner at school. He only got away from the monster by chewing garlic and breathing in its face. When his mother asked why he didn't get help from his teacher and friends, he explained that the dragon was invisible to everyone but himself.

Because of his make-believe stories when he was late from school, Terry got spankings. They were not invisible. Nor could his mother's broomstick be warded off with garlic. To ease the pain, Terry stuffed rags in the seat of his pants. This is how he got the nickname among his friends of "Padded-pants."

One day, Terry's mother told him to be on time from school so he could help her with the housework.

"I won't be late, mom," he promised, and off to school he went with his usual lunch of homemade barley bread.

When Terry got to his school, there was a note on the door from his teacher, Mr. Mootz.

"Boys, there is no school today. I have gone to the grassy area on the hill by the lake to hear the Great Teacher. Perhaps he is the Messiah we studied about in class. Join me there for extra credit, if you wish."

Terry and the other boys were happy. Except for a few who wanted the extra credit, they decided to go fishing.

"I can have a fun day," thought Terry, "and still be home on time."

After fishing for a while with his friends and not catching anything, Terry walked by himself down the lake's shoreline, and caught some small fish about the size of sardines.

"I'll save these fish for mom," he reasoned. "I may need a peace offering in case she decides to spank me."

It was shortly after noon when Terry started back home by himself. He decided to get a head start on his housework.

After walking along the shoreline, Terry took a shortcut through the grassy fields leading to the hillside. After a while, he heard a murmuring sound like bees on a blossoming tree. As he got closer to the sound he realized it wasn't the sound of bees but rather people, thousands of people dotting the hillside like wildflowers. He climbed a rock to see better. He heard a man with a booming voice say, "Blessed are you who are merciful." He liked the words of the man and wished his mother could hear him.

"This is where Mr. Mootz is," Terry thought. "Maybe I can find him and get my extra credit."

As Terry was searching for his teacher among the crowd, a man approached him.

"Can you help us, son?" asked the man.

"What's your name?" asked the boy.

"My name is Andrew. My master has need of food. Won't you share your lunch with the hungry people?"

Remembering the words he had just heard and feeling sorry for the hungry people, Terry offered his lunch.

"All I have is this barley bread which is probably stale by now. And you can have the fish, too."

At this point, Mr. Mootz came up to Terry.

"Mr. Mootz, am I glad to see you! Do I get extra credit for being here?"

"Anyone who shares his bread with the hungry gets more than extra credit with God," said the wise old teacher, who made a lesson out of most things.

Terry and Mr. Mootz listened to the Great Teacher and watched him take the bread, say a blessing and begin to divide it. The twelve men who stood beside the Great Teacher filled baskets with the bread and gave it to the people who were sitting on the grass.

"Does all that bread come from the five loaves I gave to Andrew?" asked the puzzled Terry.

"Yes," answered his teacher.

"If I tell my mom about this, she will give me a spanking for sure. She will think I am making up stories about magic."

"Just tell your mom that a Great Prophet is with us. God feeds His People just like he did in the desert."

Terry was excited. He sensed being part of history. He ate some of "his" bread and was surprised by its freshness.

After everyone had eaten, Terry helped Andrew collect leftovers. There was so much left that he was given some to take to his mother. He ran home as fast as he could.

"Mom, look what I brought you! Bread for a month!"

Terry's mother did not smile. She went to the corner of the house to get her broom. She had one thing on her mind, a spanking for a child who made up stories.

"Bend over, son. I taught you not to beg, steal or lie. Now it seems you've done at least two of the three."

"But mom, I didn't lie or beg or steal."

Terry began to cry, something he only did when he was telling the truth and his mom didn't believe him.

As his mom was about to come down with the broomhandle, Mr. Mootz came into the house.

"Don't hit him," warned the teacher. "Your son tells the truth this time. The Great Prophet, Jesus, has rewarded you because he shared his lunch with the hungry."

My son with rag-stuffed pants share? I suppose the next thing you'll tell me is he killed a dragon with garlic!"

Mr. Mootz commanded Terry's mother to listen. Then he told her about the Great Teacher who taught mercy and love, who shared the bread she had made. Then he gave her a piece of the barley bread to eat.

"This is my bread," she said. "But it's fresh, just like it came out of the oven. I baked mine last night. Tell me the secret of the Great Teacher's baking."

"I will tell you more than that," promised Mr. Mootz.

In the days that followed, Terry never again stuffed his pants with padding. There were no spankings. He had no need to make up fictional stories to get out of trouble. What he experienced on the hillside was greater than anything he could have imagined.

At school, Terry became known as "paddedlunch" because he always had a little extra bread for others. Some days he went hungry, but he always felt good about his "extra credit" with God.

LaBerge Muren

A Lesson For Bighead

HE SEEMED TO HAVE the head of an adult right from birth. His mother, who naturally loved him, named him "Mick" after her favorite Disney character, Mickey Mouse. But very few others thought he was cute. So he got the nickname "Bighead."

Bighead was an intelligent mouse. But because he was so smart, he began to think of himself as better than others. When his brothers and sisters asked him to play "hide-and-squeak," he refused. He always thought normal playing was too childish. Little by little Bighead became a snob. He ate by himself and became a loner. "I don't need friends," he would say.

Bighead and his family lived underneath the old wooden schoolhouse. It was really a nice place for mice because the children would always leave them food. The end of a peanut butter sandwich would often feed their family for a week.

The thing that Bighead liked best about living under the schoolhouse was the opportunity it gave him to learn bigger words. While his brothers and sisters were playing, he would sit and listen for hours to the lessons of the school teacher. But sadly, the only reason he wanted to learn big words was to confuse his family. He thought he could have power over the other mice by confusing them with giant words like "mareseatoatsand - doeseatoatsandlittlelambseativy.

One day as Bighead was listening to the school teacher, he heard the story of the Church Mouse. From the story, he got the idea that he, too, should travel to a church for a new adventure. So, without even a kiss goodbye to his mother, he left his home under the schoolhouse to live across the street in the Church of the Silver Dollar.

Bighead loved his first few days in the church. The Reverend who gave the sermons used many big words, words even bigger than those of the school teacher. He learned words like "armageddon" and "beelzebub."

The only bad thing about life in the church was that people didn't leave any peanut butter sandwich bits to munch on. So, Bighead went home every week to try out his big words on his family and get a good meal in his tummy. He just couldn't develop a taste for the leather in the church organ.

Every time he came home Bighead explained to his family that since he was a church mouse, they all had to show him great respect. By this he meant they had to save him the best snacks left by the children and call him by the title: "Knower of the Unknown."

"Why must we call you Knower of the Unknown?" asked his little brother. "What do you know that we don't know?"

"I know about the things that your eyes cannot see," explained Bighead.

"Whatever is he talking about?" said his sister.

Little by little Bighead began to talk more to his family. But he never had a conversation with them. Instead, he always preached to them. One evening when he had just come back from church, he preached to them about "The Great Abomination."

"The Great Abomination," he explained, "is the cat. The cat has been our enemy and made us suffer. This fleabitten feline, this miserable meower, has no right to terrorize our territory."

Bighead went on and on about the cat. The longer he spoke, the bigger became his words.

Now, it was a rule for the mice who lived beneath the old wooden schoolhouse that they were never to stand directly beneath the knothole in the ceiling of their home (which was the floor of the classroom). Bighead broke this rule and stood directly under the knothole. It was evening and the janitor was cleaning the classroom and had the light on. The light came through the knothole and acted like a spotlight for Bighead. And Bighead loved to be in the spotlight.

Bighead was ten minutes into his speech about the cat when suddenly, his light was cut off.

"Who turned off my light?" asked Bighead. "The janitor can't be finished yet."

Though Bighead bragged that he knew the unseen things of the world, he didn't know that what cut off his light was the paw of the cat reaching through the knothole directly at him. Swoop! In a second he was gone.

"He's been taken up to heaven," said his mother.

His father, who was more down-to-earth, said "I think he will be dinner for cat."

A day passed and everyone thought cat had eaten Bighead. Then as suddenly as he was snatched away, Bighead appeared to his family. Everyone was happy to see him, even though he had been such a conceited pain.

"Cat was just about to eat me," he told his family, "when I told him he would get indigestion. I told him everything I learned about how the stomach works. He began to feel sick and let me go."

"You sure taught him a lesson," said one of Bighead's cousins.

"No, I learned a lesson," said Bighead.

All the mice looked at each other in disbelief when Bighead said he "learned" from cat. They asked him what he meant.

"I learned that there's something more important in life than gathering up bigger and bigger words. I learned that you, my brothers and sisters, are the most important things in my life and that a little word like "love" is really more important than all of those big words I've been using... Anyone want to play hide and squeak?"

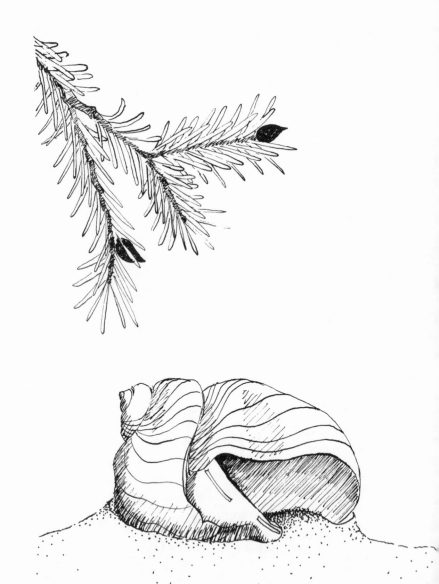

LaBerge Muren

The
Hyena's
Shell

ONCE THERE WERE seven animals who called themselves "Family." They were Fox, Giraffe, Bluebird, Beaver, Owl, Lion and Hyena. They lived in the Peaceful Forest with Lion as their fatherly leader.

One day Lion didn't feel well because he had a toothache. He decided to go away for a vacation until he felt better.

"My children," said Lion to his family, "I'm going away until I feel better. You know how grouchy I am when I have a toothache. You will get along all right if you help each other."

Right after Lion left Peaceful Forest, Hyena showed the animals something he had buried — a large sea shell. He told the animals that Lion had given him the shell to keep in touch — the shell was a kind of "hotline" between Lion and himself. This, of course, was a lie, but the animals didn't know any better.

Hyena invited the animals to listen to the shell. It did have a sound, a roaring noise. Hyena told them the noise was really Lion speaking.

"If this is Lion speaking, why can't we understand what he is saying?" asked Owl.

"That's easy to answer," said Hyena. "Lion gave me the shell. I am the only one given the power to understand him."

The animals, except for Owl, believed Hyena because they had never seen a shell and didn't know better.

"If Lion is talking to you through the shell, what is he saying?" asked Bluebird.

"I'm glad you asked," said Hyena. "Lion is saying that I am the one now in charge. You must bow before me three times a day and gather all my food."

Owl tried to tell everyone that Hyena was a hoax. But they chose to believe Hyena. After all, he had a shell with the roaring noise.

Every day the animals bowed before Hyena and gathered his food. And every day Hyena gave the animals a message from Lion. The message was always the same: "Obey Hyena."

One day, as the animals were out collecting food for Hyena, the skies grew dark. Suddenly, there was thunder and lightning. The lightning struck the Peaceful Forest and caused a fire. They remembered Lion's safety rule: "When there is a fire, follow the creekbed."

The animals followed the creekbed and Hyena went with them. But the further they went, the more nervous Hyena got.

After a day of walking, the animals found themselves by a great body of water.

"Wow," said Beaver, "This is the biggest dam I've ever seen."

Hyena looked at Beaver with disgust and said, "Beaver, this is not a dam. This is the ocean."

Beaver swam out into the ocean and a few minutes later returned with something in his flappers. It was a shell exactly like Hyena's.

Fox examined the shell and gave it to Owl. All the animals looked at each other while Beaver swam out for more shells. Suddenly, everyone realized that Hyena was a phony when they placed their newly-found shells to their ears. They knew now that the roaring noise of the shell was really the sound of the ocean and not Lion's voice to Hyena.

Owl was the first to speak to Hyena. He had a trick of his own as he said, "Hyena, my shell tells me that Lion is coming back and you have to face him."

Hyena knew he was in big trouble. He turned his tail and ran — smack into Lion who had also followed the creekbed.

"Why are you running?" asked Lion.

Hyena was so embarrassed that for the first time in his life he wished he was an ostrich so he could hide his head in the sand. He had no answer for Lion. He went back with him to face the rest of the Family.

The animals told Lion what had happened — how Hyena tried to fool everyone with the shell.

"Hyena is a fool," said Lion to his family. "But you were also foolish to have believed him."

Lion allowed Hyena to stay with the family as long as he gave up his lying ways.

LaBerge Muren

The Inch Mouse

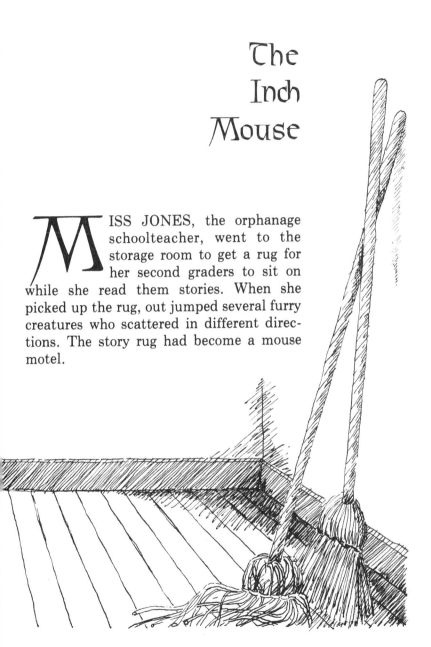

MISS JONES, the orphanage schoolteacher, went to the storage room to get a rug for her second graders to sit on while she read them stories. When she picked up the rug, out jumped several furry creatures who scattered in different directions. The story rug had become a mouse motel.

Miss Jones returned to her classroom and told the children about her problem.

"I'm sorry, children. But a family of mice was using the rug for its home. We'll have to get it cleaned before we can use it for storytime."

Meanwhile, back in the storage room, a baby mouse, named Morris, did not make his escape. He was like a new-born bird who had fallen from his nest. Something was wrong with his legs so he couldn't run. He had to drag himself along the cement floor a little bit at a time. With all his effort he seemed to get nowhere — and squeaked for help, but all of his family had run for their lives leaving him to his own luck.

Within minutes a mouse did come by. It was Milton Moss-back, the T.V. mouse. Milton did advertising for Cheese Critters, a popular snack food. While most city mice had to worry about their next meal, Milton had boxes and boxes of Cheese Critters. He was like a millionaire among mice.

When Milton saw Morris struggling to walk, he said, "How disgusting! Such a dirty creature full of lint! He crawls like a beggar! He deserves to be food for a cat!"

After these words, Milton passed by Morris without even offering to help him. He could have picked him up with his mouth and dragged him to safety. But, he couldn't be bothered.

After Milton left, Raymond Rat came into the storage room. Raymond was a troublemaker who tried to get other mice to join his group. The members of his group, his "comrats" as he called them, went around stealing from rich mice like Milton. Raymond always talked about a "ratsvolution," which meant he wanted to be the one with all the cheese.

When Raymond saw Morris dragging himself along the floor, he, too, was disgusted.

"A weak creature like that is useless in my gang. The

cheese of the world belongs to the strong," he boasted. He walked out of the storage room.

Morris paid little attention to Milton and Raymond. He had only one thing in mind — to get out of the storage room, and find his family. He had no time to think about his handicap. With a great effort he dragged himself across the floor.

After a half hour of great struggle he reached the doorway, only to find himself smack against a great furry body a hundred times his size. Morris froze. He couldn't think or pray or move. Fear took hold of every bone in his little body. His instinct, passed on to him by generations of mice, told him that he was in the paws of the world's best mousetrap — the cat. He closed his eyes and waited for his execution.

After waiting for an eternal minute with nothing happening, Morris opened his eyes and looked up. He saw the smiling face of Felina, the orphans' cat. Felina, it seems, was a gentle cat — probably like the one Noah chose for his Ark. She had been adopted by the orphans several years ago when she was a back alley wanderer. She immediately liked Morris and said to herself, "This is the first mouse I've met who hasn't run away from me. He's kind of cute — the way he moves along a little by little."

The gentle cat picked up Morris and carried him to her bowl of milk. After he had his fill, she gave him a bath as though he was one of her own kittens.

When the children came out of Miss Jones' classroom, they saw Felina licking her newly-adopted mouse. One of the children said she actually heard Morris meow like a kitten.

The children were allowed to bring the little mouse with Felina to their classroom on story days. Once when Miss Jones read them the story of Inchworm, they all looked at their pet mouse. Because he had learned to get around an inch at a time with his bad legs, they decided to call him their Inchmouse.

Stories and Parables
for Ministry

from  Resource Publications, Inc.

WINTER DREAMS and Other Such Friendly Dragons
by Joseph J. Juknialis
Paperbound $7.95
87 pages, 6" x 9"
ISBN 0-89390-010-9
This book of 15 dramas, fairy tales and fables dances with images that spark into clarity old and treasured principles. Discover the blessings concealed in "If Not For Our Unicorns" and "In Search Of God's Tracks." Especially good for retelling is the Advent story, "Sealed With A Dream."

WHEN GOD BEGAN IN THE MIDDLE
by Joseph J. Juknialis
Paperbound $7.95
101 pages, 6" x 9"
ISBN 0-89390-027-3
Here is fantasy adventure for young and old alike. In this collection of stories, find out what lies "Twixt Spring and Autumn" and "Why Water Lost Her Color". Meet Greta and Andy, whose mountain is "Carved Out of Love."

A STILLNESS WITHOUT SHADOWS
by Joseph J. Juknialis
Paperbound $7.95
75 pages, 6" x 9"
ISBN 0-89390-081-8
This collection contains 13 new stories, including: "The Cup," "The Golden Dove," "Bread that Remembers," "Golden Apples," "Pebbles at the Wall," and "Lady of the Grand." You'll find an appendix that tells you how to use the stories in church, school, or at home.

ANGELS TO WISH BY: A Book of Story-Prayers
by Joseph J. Juknialis
Paperbound $7.95
136 pages, 6" x 9"
ISBN 0-89390-051-6
A delight to read as a collection of stories, as well as a book well suited for use in preparing liturgies and paraliturgical celebrations. Scripture references, prayers, and activities that show how these story-prayers can be put to practical use in your church situation accompany most of the stories.

NO KIDDING, GOD, WHERE ARE YOU?
Parables of Ordinary Experience
by Lou Ruoff
Paperbound $7.95
100 pages, 5½" x 8½"
ISBN 0-89390-141-5
Gifted storyteller, Fr. Ruoff, helps find God for those who sometimes feel that he is hiding. These 25 stories work as effective homilies and are great for your planning — they are accompanied by Scripture references according to each season of the liturgical year.